THE YORKSHIRE TERRIER

This diminutive but stout-hearted and extremely attractive breed has been steadily increasing in popularity. For all those who have found their ideal pet in a 'Yorkie', Col. Whitehead has written a thoroughly practical and comprehensive book of guidance on rearing, care, breeding and training for the home and show ring.

General Editor: CHRISTINA FOYLE

The cover photograph shows Lilyhill Morag, owned by Mrs Lowrie.
                    Photo: D. J. Conacher

Foyles Handbooks for dog lovers

THE AIREDALE TERRIER
ALSATIANS
THE BASSET HOUND
THE BEAGLE
BOXERS
BREEDING FROM YOUR POODLE
CAIRN TERRIERS
CLIPPING YOUR POODLE
COCKER SPANIELS
COLLIES
DACHSHUNDS
DALMATIANS
DOG BREEDING
DOGS
GOLDEN RETRIEVERS
GREAT DANES
GREYHOUNDS
GRIFFONS BRUXELLOIS
IRISH TERRIERS
KING CHARLES SPANIELS
LABRADORS
THE OLD ENGLISH SHEEPDOG
PEKINGESE
POODLES
PUGS
THE SCOTTISH TERRIER
SEALYHAM TERRIERS
THE SHETLAND SHEEPDOG
SHOWING YOUR DOG
SMOOTH FOX TERRIERS
TRAINING YOUR DOG
WELSH CORGIS
WEST HIGHLAND WHITE TERRIERS
WHIPPETS
WIRE FOX TERRIERS
YORKSHIRE TERRIERS

THE
YORKSHIRE
TERRIER

HECTOR F. WHITEHEAD

W. & G. FOYLE LTD.
119-125 CHARING CROSS ROAD
LONDON, W.C.2

First published 1961
Reprinted 1963
Reprinted 1964
Reprinted 1965
Reprinted 1966
Reprinted 1967
Reprinted 1969

PRINTED IN GREAT BRITAIN
BY HOLLEN STREET PRESS LTD
SLOUGH

To

MISS CHRISTINA FOYLE

A dog lover in herself, and one of a family who have done so much to bring the various breeds of our four-footed friends before the public in such an interesting way.

Contents

1	HISTORY OF THE YORKSHIRE TERRIER	11
2	THE STANDARD EXPLAINED	17
3	BUYING A PUPPY	22
4	CARE OF THE YORKIE	26
5	WHEN YOUR YORKIE IS ILL	29
6	BREEDING	34
7	TO SHOW OR NOT TO SHOW	41
8	TRAINING ON A LEAD	50
9	REGISTRATION AND OWNERSHIP	55
10	THE YORKIE AS A COMPANION	59
11	THE RISE OF THE YORKIE	62
12	THE YORKIE IN SCOTLAND	69
13	THE YORKIE IN AMERICA	71
	APPENDIX I – RECORDS	73
	APPENDIX II – YORKSHIRE TERRIER CLUBS	74
	GLOSSARY	74
	INDEX	76

List of Illustrations

1	Huddersfield Ben	*facing page* 32
2	Rosebank Rosette	32
3	Ch. Prim	32
4	Lilyhill Joanna	33
5	Lilyhill Gem of Hintonwood	33
6	Kim, a Yorkie companion *par excellence*	33
7	Two American Yorkie puppies, clearly intelligent animals!	33
8	The best toy team group at the International Kennel Club Chicago Show 1961	48
9	Two delightful champions from the United States	48
10	Alice Scott, Mabel Ennis with Ch. Lady Roberts of Marcrakit, Judge Col. Ed. McQuown, Mrs Gordon and Ch. Star Twilight of Clu-Mor	48
11	Ch Hampark Dandy. Best of Breed at Crufts, 1961	49
12	Six champions, all owned by the late Mrs Crookshank	49

CHAPTER I

History of the Yorkshire Terrier

IT WAS NOT until 1886 that the Kennel Club decided to acknowledge this breed, under the name of Yorkshire Terrier. By that time the breed was producing a very definite type, and much as we know the Yorkie today – the picture of daintiness. Although a toy, he has the quite clear characteristics of the Terrier, and to my mind that is what makes him such a delightful character, and companion. How he was produced is fairly clear although a great deal of mystery has been built up about it, as well as many acrimonious disputes.

When the great Industrial Revolution took place, and this came over a number of years, many of the Scots from the Industrial belt of Scotland, and especially from the West, drifted down into Yorkshire and Lancashire. They had to follow work and also were always eager to better themselves. Dr Gordon Stables, a well-known writer of these days has a brick to throw at the Scots for disowning the dog, and does so in a very satirical way. So he would be aware that there was a terrier called the Paisley Terrier, otherwise the Clydesdale Terrier. We must always keep in view that dogs were not named and classified so accurately in 1860 as they were in 1960, so, having agreed on that, we can start to trace out the origin of this great little dog, and those who brought him to the front. So many writers have referred to him that it is essential to try to get them all into proper focus, and then we will find that they are all fairly well agreed.

I give the full pedigree of the great 'Huddersfield Ben' (*See* page 16) and while he was whelped in 1865, his pedigree gives at least five to ten years earlier for the breed being first noted. From the inbreeding in the pedigree it is clear that someone had an idea of what would emerge in course of time. A pedigree means a lot (or nothing) to one who has time to read and study. We are indebted for this information to Mr Frank Pearse, Faversham, who produced the first Kennel Club Stud Book in 1874 'at great and necessary expense, to fill up a blank in the history of the canine world'. He gave the first show we could accurately trace at Newcastle, 1859, purely for sporting dogs, but it is quite likely, and indeed probable, that shows of a kind were held before this date. Our ancestors were 'sporting people' who put dogs to fight monkeys, to kill rats in a given time (and our friend Ben above was an expert here) and to bait bulls.

At Birmingham, in 1860, 'Toy Terriers' appear, under five pounds.

In 1862, at Islington, appeared 'Scotch Terriers' under six pounds, and this must be kept in view.

Then next year we get a little nearer as at Cremorne, London, we get White Scotch, Fawn Scotch and Blue Scotch, two sizes in each, under seven and over seven pounds. Amongst the 'Blues' we find Mr Platt's 'Mossy' which is No 3628 in the 'Yorkie' part of the Stud Book, under seven pounds. The colour and weight are noteworthy.

In the same year 'Broken-Haired' Terriers appeared at Birmingham, and Mr Eden's 'Albert' and 'Prince' did the winning, and went in to the Stud Book.

In 1864, at Islington, Mr Dinsdale's 'Phin' won in the Scotch Terrier Class, being followed by the above two dogs, and all over seven pounds.

Up to Birmingham come 'Albert' and 'Prince' to win as 'Scotch or Broken-haired' terriers, with uncut ears, while 'Phin' above is third with cut ears.

In 1865, at Birmingham, they are simply called 'Broken-haired' terriers, and Eden's 'Don' and 'Jerry' are the winners.

So the shows went on, the nomenclature varying as 'Scotch', 'Scotch and Broken-haired' and 'Broken-haired', but in 1869, Birmingham dropped the 'Scotch', the winners being Crossley's 'Crib' and 'Jimmy', both in the Stud Book.

This year made history, as at Manchester, in December, the

great 'Huddersfield Ben' made his first appearance and was placed second as a 'Scotch' Terrier, ears cut, there being no class for 'Broken-haired'. He appeared in Mr Foster's name but at the Crystal Palace next year, he got his full name and appeared under Mrs Foster's. This lady was to make a great name for herself in the breed, and a place for it just as great. It is very difficult to estimate the debt the present day exhibitor owes to her.

At Manchester, in 1870, Foster's 'Bruce' and Inman's 'Benson' (a son of 'Huddersfield Ben') beat him into third place as 'Scotch Terriers' with cut ears. Strange to say Glasgow gave no classes for any of these terriers, so that they were not known in their own country, as Dr Gordon Stables hinted.

At Edinburgh however, 'Wattie' from Dalkeith, 'Tom' from Edinburgh, and 'Charlie' from Newcastle, did the winning as Scotch Terriers and are in the Yorkie stud pages. In the same year, 1871, the Crystal Palace and Birmingham gave classes for Broken-haired, but no Scotch.

Manchester gave 'Scotch' Terriers, and Mrs Foster swept the boards in 'Ears Cut' with 'Emperor' and 'Dundreary', and to close my record, she went over to Dublin the following year, and won with 'Dundreary' and 'Bruce' (by the great 'Ben') in 'Broken-haired' – a three day show.

So as not to be wearisome, I skip to the Manchester Show of 1873, where, in Scotch Terriers over twelve pounds, 'Dundreary' and 'Mozart' won, while Mrs Foster's 'Crack' was first in the under twelve pound group.

If the above records are to be taken at face value, at this stage, I consider there is some ground for thinking that Scotland had some part, however small, in helping to produce the Yorkie.

There is another point to be studied, in so far as this K.C. Stud Book had a group for 'Toy Terriers' (Rough and Broken-haired), and a great many of the entrants were sired by 'Huddersfield Ben', or descendants of his. To complete the confusion, Mrs Foster entered in 'Toy Terriers, broken-haired under five pounds' three who did some winning – 'Cobden', 'Little Kate' and 'Tiny', all close descendants of 'Ben'; while 'Mozart', referred to above, had a pup by the name of 'Wallet' winning at Nottingham in 1873, under the same category.

In other words puppies from the same litter might be shown as different 'breeds', and be entered in different catégories of the Stud Book. What a blessing to historians it would have been, if there had been a Kennel Club on present day lines, but still we should be glad there is so much left of the old days.

Foundations

I would say that there are few better stock breeders than the Yorkshireman, and that the Scot is not far behind. What went on in their own kennels was their own business, but other blood than the above must have been used to produce the present marvel – or should I say Little Marvel. That the above was the foundation, would appear to be beyond doubt when you study the official records.

In the Clyde Valley, there was a dog called the Paisley Terrier and by some the Clydesdale Terrier, and under the above name *he* was shown no later than 1902. Now here is what a great authority on Terriers says: 'It has been said that this terrier was originally a cross between the ordinary Skye Terrier and the Yorkshire Terrier, but, though it is of quite modern origin, no proof has been produced when such crosses took place, or who made them. To my idea it is much more likely that the Yorkshire Terriers were produced from the Paisleys or Clydesdales'.

This entirely agrees with my views, crossed with an original local Terrier in Halifax and Bradford, as there must have been such there. It is alleged that the Maltese were also used – this is where the Silver blue comes from as opposed to the Steel Blue – and that these dogs were taken into the country by sailors trading with the Mediterranean, without anyone being interested then. Quite possible but there is no evidence, though I have been given this idea at a recent show.

On the other hand, the Clydesdale was a soft coated Skye

Terrier, and its colour given as a level bright steel blue, the head, legs and feet a clear golden tan, free from grey sooty or dark hairs. I wish you to note the 'sooty' and how that word comes into the standard of our Yorkie. The parting of the coat (shedding in Scotland) extends from the head to the tail evenly down each side. What more tempting to infuse into the Yorkie of that day, nameless then, like the Scottie.

My considered opinion is therefore that the Yorkie as it stands today, is a manufactured dog, and that the above is not far from the truth, if not the truth itself. It detracts nothing from the great little fellow or those who produced him, but rather gives them credit that with the material at hand, they have succeeded in such a short time in getting the breed to come so true to type – except in size, which in my view cannot be properly controlled in any breed.

THE PEDIGREE OF HUDDERSFIELD BEN

Owner: Mrs M. A. Foster, 21 Lady Lane, Lister Hills, Bradford.

Breeder: Mr W. Eastwood, of Huddersfield.

Born: 1865. *Died:* September, 1871.

No. 3612.

Pedigree: By Mr Boscovitch's dog – out of 'Lady'.

His sire by Thomas Ramsden's 'Bounce', by his 'Bob' out of his 'Old Dolly'.

'Bob' by Haigh's 'Teddy' (from Lascelles Hall, Huddersfield) out of 'Old Dolly'.

'Teddy' by J. Swift's 'Old Crab' (from Manchester) out of Kershaw's 'Old Kitty' (from Halifax).

'Lady' by Eastwood's 'Old Ben', and granddaughter of 'Old Sandy'.

'Ben' by Ramsden's 'Bounce' out of 'Young Dolly', by 'Old Sandy' out of 'Old Dolly', by 'Albert' (from Manchester), by 'Old Soldier'.

'Old Sandy' by Haig's 'Teddy' out of Walshaw's 'Kitty', by the Healey House dog out of Walshaw's 'Pink'.

This is taken from the Kennel Club Stud Book of 1874.

It should be noted that every dog and bitch could be identified by the breeders of that date, and that there is clear evidence of considered in-breeding with Bounce, Old Sandy and Old Dolly. It will give the reader considerable interest if this pedigree is extended on the usual form. It also gives insights into breeding.

CHAPTER II

The Standard Explained

HAVING OUTLINED how the breed originated, we will now move on to the standard.

This was drawn up by the Yorkshire Terrier Club, founded in 1898, and everything possible should be done to breed to it. This may be difficult but it can be done. The bad system of changing the standard to suit certain dogs should be avoided, as it has previously worked to the great benefit of the breed.

THE OFFICIAL STANDARD

General Appearance. Should be that of a long-coated toy terrier, the coat hanging quite straight and evenly down each side, a parting extending from the nose to the end of the tail. The animal should be very compact and neat, the carriage being very upright, and having an important air. The general outline should convey the existence of a vigorous and well-proportioned body.

Head. Should be rather small and flat, not too prominent, or round in the skull, nor too long in the muzzle, with a perfect black nose. The fall on the head to be long, of a rich golden tan, deep in colour at the sides of the head about the ear roots, and on the muzzle where it should be very long. The hair on the chest a rich bright tan. On no account must the tan on the head extend on to the neck, nor must there be any *sooty* or dark hair intermingled with any of the tan.

Eyes. Medium dark and sparkling, having a sharp intelligent expression, and placed so as to look directly forward. They should not be prominent and the edge of the eyelids should be of a dark colour.

Ears. Small V-shaped, and carried semi-erect, or erect, and not far apart, covered with short hair, colour to be of a deep rich tan.

Mouth. Perfectly even, with teeth as sound as possible. An animal having lost any teeth through accident not a fault, providing the jaws are even.

Body. Very compact, and a good loin. Level on the top of the back.

Forequarters. Legs quite straight, well covered with hair of a rich golden tan a few shades lighter at the ends than at the roots, not extending higher on the forelegs than the elbow.

Hindquarters. Legs quite straight, well covered with hair of a rich golden tan a few shades lighter at the ends than at the roots, not extending higher on the hind legs than the stifle.

17

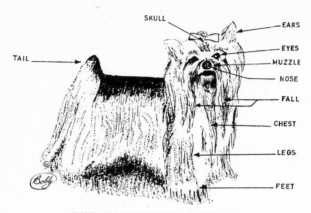

THE YORKSHIRE TERRIER

See below for Standard of points

Coat. The hair on the body moderately long and perfectly straight (not wavy), glossy, like silk, and of a fine silk texture.

Colour. A dark steel blue (not silver blue) extending from the occiput (or back of skull) to the root of the tail, and on no account mingled with fawn, bronze or dark hairs. The hair on the chest a rich bright tan. All tan hair should be darker at the roots than in the middle, shading to a still lighter tan at the tips.

Weight and Size. Weight up to seven pounds.

VALUE OF POINTS IN JUDGING

Formation and Terrier Appearance	15
Colour of Hair on Body	15
Richness of Tan on Head and Legs	15
Quality and Texture of Coat	10
Quality and Length of Coat	10
Head	10
Mouth	5
Legs and Feet	5
Ears	5
Eyes	5
Tail (Carriage of)	5
	100

Notes for beginners.

To a beginner, the standard may seem difficult to follow. It is, of course, intended purely for the exhibitor, but even if you are to keep a Yorkie solely as a companion, you should have it near the accepted goal of perfection. Actually there has been very little change down the years, though put in different words and forms. In the 'values' given to the various points, there has been no change since the first edition of *Show Dogs* by that doyen of the dog world, Theo Marples. Here is what he says of the Yorkie:

'Beautiful to look at, active as a kitten, vivacious as the most "Perky Pom", the perfect Yorkshire Terrier is the acme of Toy Dog virtue and perfection, looked at from every standpoint'.

Those who own the dog and the breed agree with that.

Now let us take the standard and see the points where we can help ourselves and the dog. Although colour printing has been brought to a very high pitch of truth, it is very expensive and I doubt if it would do justice to the shades of tan in a Yorkie. Therefore it is essential to see other dogs than your own, either with their breeders, or in the ring at shows, preferably championship ones.

Coat

This takes fifty points for colour, richness, texture and length, so here the owner can help a great deal, as will be explained later, by the use of the brush, and hair stimulants (*See* page 39). Keep in view that success here means half the battle over.

Head

Head with its items of mouth, ears, and eyes, takes another twenty-five points and, as the dog is born with these, there is not much that can be done about it. By careful study, you can see where each item fails, if it does. Expression is not referred to but this comes under the first point, and your dog should look as if it wanted to show and could do it.

Seventy-five of the points are now gathered in.

Formation and Terrier Appearance

It is worth while noting here that it is to look like a terrier which means being lively, alert and on its toes; with a keen outlook, which means not soft and sweet like the toy part of it. And a little terrier of three or four pounds can look as game and ready for a walk as any other of its kindred. You can help here by training your dog, and especially in walking gaily and proudly. Most judges now insist on the little fellow walking from and to him, and perhaps round in a circle in a procession. Training can make him shine there. I hear some exhibitors object to this, but in my view to see the little fellow trot round with his coat touching the ground, his head up and his wee legs twinkling through his coat, is enough to take seventy points from the hardest hearted judge. So here another fifteen points are accounted for.

Legs and Feet

These bring in five points, and you will note what is said under Fore and Hind Quarters. Legs must be straight and the hair should be tan to the elbow and the stifle respectively. In addition he should move them straight from back to front without any 'in-toed' appearance in front or 'cow-hocks' behind, as these faults do detract from him when moving. Indeed it detracts from him when he is standing to attention, and wondering what the judge is looking at.

Tail

Finally the tail, which brings in five points. However, in the overall picture it affects appearance, and may drop you additional points elsewhere. It should be cut to medium length (I refer to this in the puppy section), and the hair should be darker in colour than the rest of the coat. It should be carried a little higher than the level of the back, and you can help here. If your dog is healthy and happy and trusts you, his tail will never go down. When it does, it gives the little fellow the appearance of cringing, and you drop points on appearance.

The photos in the book will give you a good idea of what is wanted in appearance. Above all, *the back should be level*, as there is nothing worse than a roach back, which means a curve upwards like a bow. At the same time, he should not dip at the back which is the opposite of roach.

In short you should aim at a short, compact, well-knit dog, no matter what his size, who will stand on four firm legs and feet, with his tail at attention. The colouring of the coat speaks for itself, but the length of the coat should be to the ground or more and this applies to the 'fall' and moustaches. I give some wonderful records on page 73. The weight should not exceed seven pounds, but if you can get down to three or four pounds, without losing character, you are on the road to success in the ring.

CHAPTER III

Buying a Puppy

WHEN I WAS an apprentice to a legal firm after leaving school, I was fortunate in that I was taught typewriting and shorthand there. Through this I became the clerk to the senior partner and I learned things then that stood me in good stead in later life. One of them was in horse dealing and if you apply this information to dog dealing, you will never be far out in buying. One client was a well-known horse dealer, and his turn-over in all classes of horses must have been tremendous, and especially in pit ponies, then very much used compared with today. From time to time he had court actions but I never knew him to lose one. If you went to him and told him that you wanted to buy a reliable horse for a certain purpose, whether for riding, for children, or for a van, and discussed price, you got what you wanted. If you asked for one safe with children, you could stake your last penny that no child would ever come to grief from that pony. If you knew all about horses and more than he did, good and well, you got value for money and the warranty you asked for, and there it ended. Perhaps, however, you did not say what you wanted, or more than you could help, so that you could buy below market price and be smart. If so, you were foolish, for very few knew as much about a horse as X did.

Now let us apply what I learned then, and believe to be right, to the Yorkie. You want a companion, male or female. For some unknown reason most people want a dog pup and ignore the loving devotion of the bitch. They say a bitch comes in season and all the dogs gather round – but never consider whose dog gathers round, and that it may be theirs who is out all night. But one or two waits until two a.m. teaches them the facts of life, and that a bitch in season has merely to be shut up until the time is over, that she seldom if ever wanders, and is always at home.

You should go to a friend who has a satisfactory companion, and find out where he got it, and do likewise. Get one about three months or so, and if you are in earnest about only wanting a companion, then say so and you will get what you want from the seller, but do not try to be smart and try to get a breeding or show specimen on false pretences. You may be dealing with a doggie 'X' like my horsey 'X' and make a bad impression. There are more honest dog sellers in the world than the other kind. You may get the best in the litter as no one *knows* how a pup will turn out, but you will at least get one that the seller can hold his face to and not get a bad name.

If at the back of your mind there is the feeling that you might breed as a hobby some time, then get a bitch, and tell the seller that while you might breed sometime in the future, you want a nice companion. You will get it, and he will keep an eye on your bitch in case any of his own do not breed and he will fall back on you – a big step in your favour.

However, perhaps you do not know anyone. Then visit a show where you may see someone showing with whom you can discuss the matter. If this fails, buy one of the weekly dog papers, in which you will find advertisements. If there are any breeders near at hand, drop a note and suggest that you call, and you will get a reply. When you call you must decide quickly whether you are to trust the seller, or buy from your own ideas – it is up to you. Prices have risen steeply in the last few years owing to the increase in the cost of food and labour, so it is not easy to fix a price, but pay the value to you. A rough guide is that a pup is always worth the cost of the service at least, so if you go in for a champion line, you would expect to pay somewhere in the neighbourhood of £10. Of course, up to a point, the older the pup is the easier it is to fix a value, as the faults begin to show – and also the good points. If you have a friend in the dog world, he should be able to get you better value.

The value of a pup was well illustrated to me years ago, when a man called one evening, and said he was told I had some Cairns and he wanted one for his wife. This was Edinburgh, and he was clearly a workman, but I had three about six months and wanted to sell two. He was quite frank and he said he wanted a good 'disposition' one as it was for his wife, he could not afford to pay more than five pounds and he knew a bitch was a better pal and guard than a dog. At that time five pounds was five pounds, and while I might get more elsewhere, I was struck with his method of gauging value as he told me that a dog was cheap at that price, as it would live Ten Years on an average and if you did not get ten shillings a year pleasure out of it, you should not have a dog – and the seven shillings and sixpence tax was nothing to do with the dog. He got what he wanted and I got the five pounds, but the profit came three years later. He arrived one night, though how he found my new address I do not know, to tell me that the bitch had her first litter, all dogs. I was very interested and went to see them. There were four dogs and he said, 'You can have two dogs for the price of the bitch and the service, if you think that reasonable'. I thought they were worth more, but he said in his blunt way, 'You treated me fairly, and I want to do the same. There will be a profit on the two left'. I think therefore I have shown that it pays in the long run to be quite frank when buying, as has been my experience over a long and happy existence with my many dog friends, and, I hope, few enemies.

On the other hand, you may be shown a litter or a group, and allowed to take you pick. For show purposes the chief points to look for are small size, shortness of back, not too heavy bone, and at four months the coat should be straight, with signs of dark tan on the head and legs. Small size should not be confused with weakness, as though small he should be bright and active. On the other hand if you want a gay companion do not be too much influenced by size, but pay more attention to the colour, as I have later (page 36) explained about puppies being born black. The puppy that comes to you wagging his little tail is always worth an extra look. My final word of warning is that no one can be sure of the size of a puppy or how it will turn out – but the opinion of an expert is always worthy of careful attention.

CHAPTER IV

Care of the Yorkie

IN THIS MATTER there is very little actual difference between the Yorkie and any other dog. They have their likes and dislikes, and as they are all about the same size, they can damage each other quite easily. The disease called jealousy can exist in a small dog as well as a large one, and must be guarded against, especially since one is inclined to think that because they are small they must be 'tame'. But remember always that the foundation of the Yorkie is 'terrier', and you know what terriers can do when roused.

I do not recommend outdoor kennels unless you are lucky enough to get hold of a house with a biggish barn and can fit it up accordingly into compartments. In that case you want heat for the winter, which should be supplied by electricity to keep the place at as near one temperature as possible. Even then I recommend that each individual has its own Cardboard Carton – as in the event of sickness and above all distemper, they can be cleared out from time to time and replaced at practically no expense, and they are warm. Failing the barn, one room in the house should be given to your Yorkies, possibly the kitchen, if it is one of the old world kind and not the modern kitchenette. You can have movable wire pens, though I would not recommend more than one dog and one bitch to each. Two of the same sex may fight, but by the time you get this number you will have learned the art of sizing up your dogs and knowing them. The above applies to those intended for breeding and companionship, and not for dogs that are being groomed for a forthcoming show.

There must be no straw about as it is death to coats. In winter when heat is needed, the Yorkies can lie on one of the many portable beds advertised which have a canvas bottom that can be laced up. With a carton over this, all will be well as the Yorkie does not require pampering. In this room should be kept the few medicines suggested in the next chapter and also brushes, and a comb for the odd case.

Remember the army blanket for the bottom of each carton. This recalls to me a dog act I once saw put on in a theatre, and I was so tickled with it that I went the next day to see if the 'lady trainer' would see me and talk. She did and was very pleased that someone had noted the spontaneity of one of the little actors. This was a Yorkie, with the furnishings kept short, who was in a separate little kennel on the stage. Whenever the other dozen or so dogs did their turn, he flew out and did it over again for them, to the great 'annoyance' of the trainer. This was all make-believe as when she told him what she thought of him and what she would do to him, he gave a little whining bark, as much as to say 'I wonder'. My point was that I thought the dog enjoyed the fun just as much as the audience, as when two ducks played see-saw, he jumped on in the middle and moved the see-saw up and down so well, that the ducks got knocked off.

She told me that most of the parts he played came to him naturally and he never had an ill word said to him, as he seemed to 'know' the spirit of the whole act. She had obtained other dogs in order to try to train them to replace him if such a sad day ever came, or to give him a rest, but she had not had much success so far. I asked if there was a price at which she would sell him and the reply was, 'You would have to buy the two of us.' So I went every night to see the imp enjoy himself, and would go a long way to see him again. He enjoyed every minute and timed himself exactly.

Remember that those that are being washed and brushed, must have special attention to ensure that they do not catch cold, as this can lead to congestion and pneumonia – and a lot of hard work in nursing, which can be avoided. If the room has a stone or concrete floor, then have boarding laid under the cartons, and a special corner spread with dry sand.

With a little patience the dogs can be trained to go there always to ease themselves.

Apropos the drying of the dog after washing, this should normally be done in front of a fire, but there is a recent development that is worth trying, and that is by using an electric hair drier. I have recently tried it on terriers on the advice of a friend and found it worked well, as terriers at times roll themselves in muck, and there is no accounting for this nor stopping them. Some of the driers have rather noisy motors, and at first your dog may be a bit shy of this, but with patience, and trust on the part of the dog, this will pass and I agree that it is quicker. Once the little fellow gets used to it, you can easily get him to stand and be brushed at the same time as the drier is finishing him off. New ideas are always worth trying at least once, and if good persevered with.

CHAPTER V

When your Yorkie is ill

SICKNESS COMES to us all at sometime or other, and unfortunately this applies to our four-footed friends too. But my advice is not to meet it half way by imagining there is something wrong and that you must get the Vet or dose him for the dog worms or something else. We have to be thankful that the average dog is healthy and if properly fed and housed, will usually remain that way. However, we are all fairly well fed and housed and still become sick. The great guide to how your dog is feeling is his tail and, after that, his eyes. The tail is usually up and usually wags, but if it is down and wagging very feeble to greet you, then there is something wrong. Of course he may have made a 'mistake' during the night and is ashamed of this, but that possibility can quickly be checked. It is common knowledge that the eye of a fish is the best guide to freshness and goodness; similarly, if the eye of your Yorkie is not sparkling also, there is something very wrong.

I will give you a bitter instance of my own. I came home about eleven p.m., and my wife said to me that the puppy had not eaten anything since the morning and she did not like this – nor did I. It then suddenly dashed out of its box, flew round the room, collapsed and died inside one minute. We were not novices but we were hurt and surprised, as we had not suspected anything wrong except lack of appetite. I took the little body to the Vet, a great friend of mine, and he remarked that as it was not often I lost a puppy, he would carry out a post mortem. This showed that a splinter of wood two inches long was imbedded in part of the intestine, and nothing we could have done would have been of any use. How the pup got this is still a mystery. This leads me to make the point that a huge collection of medicines is a very doubtful investment. With many more Vets and specific medicines available now compared with the time when each dog owner had his areca nut in his pocket and actually grated it himself counting two grains to the pound for an adult plus ten per cent of Santonine, with reduced amounts for a puppy, and it all worked out well as a dose for worms. Today many chemists stock all the leading dog medicines. Why store up, therefore, and let the drugs get old when you can get them fresh at almost any time – unless you are far from the madding crowd.

My fail-me-never is Angier's Emulsion, and if a dog looks out of sorts a dose can do no harm in any case. I found this out accidentally, as I had to take this myself for lung trouble many years ago. We had a dog in the house that was not 'too well', and he was a cute lad. I thought if this does me good it cannot harm him, so he got his dose. I pouched the cheek and it went down. He looked better the next day, the treatment was continued and he was all right within the next ten days. Probably a chill on the stomach, a diagnosis with which my Vet agreed. Remember that while a dog can digest bones, his stomach is very sensitive to a chill.

Castor oil or Liquid Paraffin should always be on hand and, where the dog shows violent thirst or vomitting, a teaspoonful will clear the stomach of any foreign bodies. This is easy to administer by pouching the cheek as explained later in this chapter.

Epsom salts are another item usually to be found in a house and easily administered. The amount needed is about what would cover the old three-penny piece.

If you are quite sure that your dog has swallowed poison, an emetic such as washing soda should be given at once, and then the Vet must come or you must go to him. There is no choice in a case like this.

Asprin is a faithful friend, and safer than many so-called tonics and sedatives. About a grain per pound weight is right for an adult, but less for a puppy. This is very useful for fits or hysteria, and is quicker acting than bromide, I think.

There was once a standby which no dogman passed over and that was *Benbow's Mixture*. I never found a dog that liked it but it undoubtedly did good, the system being to give it as a tonic, dosed for about six days and then missed for six days and then another six days dosing. It should not be given if the dog has diarrhoea. I found it very good indeed. I understand you can get it in the form of tablets now, but I have never tried them. All these remedies except the last one, are in most homes, and are hard to fault in their own limits. For anything stronger, I recommend the Vet's views.

Administering a dose can be difficult, as can showing a judge the dog's teeth. I recommend therefore that you should early on, get the puppy into the habit of having his teeth examined and his mouth opened. You slip your index finger into the mouth on one side, your thumb similarly on the other side, with your wrist placed on the dog's head. The lips turn into the mouth and the dog gives in at once. It is advisable to have someone to slip the medicine into the back of the mouth and touch the tip of the tongue, when the job is done. For pouching, your left hand holds the dog's mouth shut, and you slip the index finger of the right hand under the lip and pull the cheek gently out. Then the liquid is poured in and the head held up so that the dog must swallow. Again, it is better to have the help of a friend.

A dog does not take a 'cold' as we do, and therefore be warned that if you see a running nose, the 'fish' eye and 'matter', there is every possibility that you have a case of distemper. You can give Angier's as a temporary relief but you want the Vet at once. Keep the dog warm and a hot water bottle will not come amiss, but be much appreciated. There are so many new ideas that I leave it to the Vet to guide you.

Worms. Many people seem to think that a dog and especially a young one must have worms. That is not the case, some do and some do not, and the idea of dosing 'in case' is bad dogmanship. Know first, and if you do not then get someone who does, probably the Vet. There are now on the market pills that can be given without first starving for a period, and

I have used one type for five years now, and find it satisfactory. Of course you do not see the beastly things squirming on the ground as we used to do, but you can see that the dog is healthy and happy and cannot have many worms at the worst. I refer to *Ral Evapo* but I understand that there are others equally good, although I have not tried them.

That is the way I have always handled these two dog diseases, and I now touch on the other method, on which you must make up your own mind or be guided by your Vet. I admit frankly I am against vaccination. I think good sanitation and cleanliness count a great deal. Therefore whether you epivax or inoculate your puppies lies with you. I do not and have suffered no loss, but if the Vet came in and said it should be done, then it would be. I have my own views, but there is no use in asking advice and treatment and then refusing it.

Now for cuts and bruises: Hydrogen Peroxide is very good, and of course there are many other patent washes which you may have used. For cuts, whether caused by other dogs, thorns, glass or such like, wash out with a weak solution, and if the dog is upset, warm the water. If it is a bad gash, get the Vet. For the head, ears, and eyes, you want help and great care, or irretrievable damage may be done, through unskilled bandaging.

For broken bones, call the Vet as soon as possible. You can get them now, but in my young days, you might have to go forty or fifty miles for one, and there were no cars. The Vet can set a leg perfectly. I knew of a case where a Saluki broke its shoulder blade and I thought it was hopeless to attempt to make her perfect again and said so. I swallowed my words with pleasure, as the Vet operated, then wired it up. The dog and I became great friends as I took a turn at watching that it lay quiet for the first few weeks. It healed perfectly and she won two challenge certificates afterwards. She never forgot me, for at one show I stood, looked at her and said 'Hullo'; the head came up, and a paw was offered, to the great pleasure of the new owner.

You may get skin trouble though I think it is not so often

By courtesy of Dennis Marples, 'Our Dogs

1. Huddersfield Ben

Photo: Thomas Fall

2. Rosebank Rossette. A typical brood bitch.

3. Ch. Prim, an excellent specimen of Yorkie.

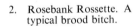

4. Lilyhill Joanna, weight 2¼ lb, now in Alaska.

5. Lilyhill Gem of Hintonwood, weight 3 lb. notable for his long moustaches.

6. Kim, a Yorkie companion *par excellence*.

7. *Below:* Two American Yorkie puppies, clearly intelligent animals!

Photo: *Glenview Studio*

seen as in the old days. Fleas come from nowhere, and lice can be very troublesome if not noted early. Your Vet or Chemist can always tell you what is the position in preventatives at the moment, and if you buy one of the weekly dog papers, which I strongly recommend you should, you will find many advertisements and usually one or two experts giving you their guidance. D.D.T. is very good in its many preparations but you must be careful if the skin is broken. Eczema is more common than mange, but if you suspect the latter and expecially in the ear, then your Vet is the man to handle it. A simple dressing for any skin trouble is equal parts of paraffin and olive oil, thickened to the consistency of thick cream with flowers of sulphur and rubbed into the bad spot. This keeps things under control until you are sure what is wrong, and the treatment may lead to complete recovery. I used it for years. On no account should advertised cures be poured into the ears, as this is a delicate part of the dog and you do not want to risk making him deaf, when it can be avoided.

CHAPTER VI

Breeding

WE HAVE A GREAT DEAL to learn yet about breeding in dogs, and also the effect of the ancestors in improving, or otherwise, the progeny. Whether a bitch should be bred from on her first 'season' or not is a very debatable point, but I think it would be better to wait for the second 'season' in Yorkies and thus give the bitch time to mature. Then there is the question of size in the brood bitch. Four to five lbs may be taken as a useful average, and by using a smaller stud dog (having studied the pedigrees of both) there is every hope of small healthy puppies, and an easy time for the mother. The decision however always lies with the owner of the bitch. Sending a bitch to a Champion dog as sire may turn out all right, but it may not, though usually it means puppies that will sell on their name.

On the other hand, it is much better, having decided on the dog that you think is to suit and improve your stock, to go and see it, if you have not already done so. See that you have the blood of the dog you admire, on both sides of the prospective pup, and never forget that a pup has a dam as well as a sire. In other words if the pups are not good, do not, please, blame the champion sire, as the person responsible for the mating is you. Do not be afraid to send your bitch to a distance in a warm box, as you will find the Yorkie breeders are a kindly and friendly lot, and will be as good to your dog as to their own.

One word of warning, you pay for the service, but no one can guarantee pups – so if there is a miss, either or both parties may be to blame. The owner of a stud dog will do everything to ensure pups for the sake of his own name and that of the dog, but he is not infallible. If the bitch misses, there is no legal claim to a free service later on – unless that condition is made before the service. It is usually given as an act of grace and sympathy, but only that.

Whelping

After service feeding should be carefully studied. The bitch should be fed twice a day and a 'meaty' bone will not come amiss as a titbit.

Exercise her as regularly as the weather will permit, and if not suitable, then encourage her to play with toys indoors.

You can get tables to tell you when the bitch should whelp and so long as they give this merely as a guide, good and well, but the exact day and hour is always uncertain. My own idea was to keep a careful eye, night and morning, from and after the sixtieth day, and if there were no signs on the sixty-third day, I always called the Vet, no matter how much I fancied my experience. Err on the side of safety in such a small and dainty breed, but never lose sight of the fact that reproducing their species is quite a natural event, and neither a disease nor an accident.

If things go wrong, the cooler you keep, the less nervous the little dog is. Once the first puppy arrives, the rest usually follow, and the less interference with the mother the better. The main thing to see is that each one is suckling, and that you praise and pat the mother.

On the question of feeding, so many new ideas and foods have come into existence that some old ideas are forgotten or ignored, but there is one old fashioned idea I decline to give up. It is both simple and effective. Often when a bitch was whelping and always when it was over, she got a drink of 'Gruel' the old-fashioned, north country fail-me-never. It is still worth remembering and does not entail having a medicine chest. Put a handful of oatmeal in a bowl. Pour boiling water over it, stirring well all the time until it is like thick cream. Put in a pinch of salt. Add a pat of fresh butter, and stir till melted. Pour in fresh milk to blood heat. Stir finally and tip with your tongue to ensure it is the right heat. I have never met a case yet of failure to enjoy this, and then comes the satisfaction of sleep, with the puppies snuggling round, all content.

I recommend whelping indoors, in kitchen or a spare room, where it is warm. Boxes are not easy to get, and recently I have seen the cardboard carton put to excellent use for whelping. Your grocer will be delighted to give you some, and you can cut and adjust to your own ideas. Then they can be replaced so easily, that they are always clean, and so light to move about. For the actual whelping I recommend clean sacking, which can be burnt afterwards and replaced by clean warm *material*. I find army blankets, cut to size, very convenient, easily obtained from advertisements, and reasonably cheap.

Rearing (early)

The puppies start to eat on their own when roughly four weeks old, and usually start on the dish their dam eats from. This should consist of milk pudding, cornflower or similar light food. Any food fit for babies will suit them and they gradually go on to adult food. Usually they should not suckle the dam after six weeks from birth. You will see that she gets irritated before this time, so provide a 'perch' where she can lie and look down on her offspring without their being able to come up and annoy her. Indeed, you can have this waiting her from three weeks.

Now for a shock! Your Yorkie puppies are born *black*, and those which are blackest later often turn out the best so far as coat and colouring are concerned. Do not let this worry you in the least, and you will enjoy the novelty of the transformation of colour as the months go by.

Foster Mothers

Here we must stay a minute and consider the dark side. Unfortunately bitches can die whelping, milk fever can occur, and puppies can fade away; you can do nothing and even the Vet may fail. This is the time when the breeder can help the bitch and the Vet, by coolness and control of nerves, in facing the inevitable. There is nothing more tragic than to see a little pet pass on, without being able to help. You will find in the Dog Press kennels that advertise *foster mothers* and I would recommend that contact be kept with the owner of one of these, ready for the emergency of a litter too big for the dam, or illness on her side. Of course the Vet should be there and he may be able to suggest where a foster can be found.

There are Vets now who specialise almost entirely in dogs, and our four-footed friends have a far better chance of recovery than when I was a boy. Vets were then very much fewer, and handled farm stock more than anything else.

Rearing and training

The little 'black' puppies are now over six weeks, and unless they are to be kept for show or breeding purposes, I would suggest that, either alone or in consultation with an expert friend, you should consider which you are likely to retain, so commencing the long uphill struggle to produce the 'flier'. Those not to be kept should be sold at about three months of age, when the final decisions on retention are made.

Before this there are one or two things to be seen to. Examine each pup carefully for *dew claws*, these being rudimentary toes on the inside of the hind legs. They are easily removed with sharp scissors, causing little pain. Iodine applied after cutting removes any risk of infection and the mother's tongue does the rest. Then at the same time (three to six days) the tail should be *docked*. Once learned, this is a simple operation, but I would recommend the novice to have the Vet for the first time, and even subsequently as it affects the appearance of the little fellow so much. On the underside of the tail there is tan from the root outwards, which can be seen when you turn him on his back. You follow the tan and make the cut just inside the black. Read the Standard on tails. My advice always is to see these two operations, which are minor, done by the Vet or an Expert friend, before you tackle them yourself. Thanks to the Government, there is now no *cropping* of ears, though this is still practised on the Continent and in America. Barbarous.

When the puppy is three or four months old the change in colour begins to take place, down the sides, legs, etc. The back may remain black till almost a year old in some cases, and the full beauty of colour takes two or even three years to fully mature. The slow maturer is usually a laster.

Up to the age of eight or nine months nothing more is needed than daily brushing and combing, with a *wash* being given every two or three weeks and steadily stiffening up to once a week. If this is done systematically, the dog gets used to the operation and then comes to like it. While any Yorkie will grow a good coat, it needs help to make it extra good as to colour and length. Special preparations used to be rubbed and brushed into the coat, and every kennel has its own secrets. *Neatsfoot òil* is very good, and indeed if you apply this from three months, you cannot do any harm. Do not use Nylon brushes, but the ordinary 'Baby' brush. This will always apply, but you may also have to comb at times, care being taken not to break the hairs, and special attention paid to knots.

After the first birthday and even before, weekly washing is essential, and White Windsor Soap has stood the test of time, giving a good lather and cleanse. When finally rinsing out, the water should be poured along the top of the back from the head to tail, exactly in the middle so that the coat falls down each side evenly. Then it is carefully dried, rubbing gently downwards, with a soft towel so as not to ruffle or snarl the coat, and to avoid cracking it. When thoroughly dry, the coat may be rolled up in soft tissue paper, and fixed with a thin elastic band so as not to let it get dirty or damaged. This is done only when long enough, special attention then also being paid to the 'fall' and 'moustaches'. Dogs *will* scratch, spoil·a day's work, and do irreparable damage. To avoid this, it is customary to have 'bootees' for the hind feet. I think wash leather is best, but linen or cotton can be used, but not flannel owing to the hairs. The rolling up applies specially to the fall and moustaches – I saw one the other day that could not be less than a foot long, when brushed out. These must be tied up when eating, though some breeders use a cloth mask, which is easily made at home. The fall and

moustaches may be plaited as, well as rolled up. The ears
are often covered with a wealth of coat as the dog matures,
which may take two years or more.

Feeding

During this period, feeding has to be watched carefully as it
is very important. While a normal coat is not too difficult to
grow, it must have something to anchor on. The stomach
should never be allowed to become constipated, and a little
liquid paraffin is good, but only when needed. Do not pamper
and avoid turning your dog into a tricky feeder. Milk is good
from the start; bread soaked in gravy; tripe; fish (be careful
about the bones); liver; and if you have it at any time, a bit
of chicken, together with all the skin.

If your dog likes vegetables, by all means let him have them,
but never forget the fact that the dog was and is a flesh-eating
animal.

Preparations for the Coat

As I said earlier, every kennel has its own specifics and
I give two here from old time specialists:

Rawdon Lee recommended the following:

Tincture of Cantharides	1 oz.
Oil of Rosemary	$\frac{1}{2}$ oz.
Bay Rhum	$\frac{1}{4}$ pint
Olive Oil	$\frac{1}{2}$ pint
White Precipitate	1 Drachm

This should be carefully mixed and rubbed into the roots
of the hair once a week, and thoroughly brushed out. Take
care not to crack or curl the hair.

Robert Leighton gives a recipe of Sam Jessop who was a
great light in the Yorkshire world in the old days:

Hydrous Wool Fat	2 oz.
Benzoated Lard	2 oz.
Almond Oil	2 oz.
Phenol	30 gr.
Alcohol (90%)	$\frac{1}{2}$ oz.

The first three ingredients are melted together upon a water-bath; the phenol, dissolved in the alcohol, being added when nearly cold; the whole being thoroughly mixed together.

Either are worth trying but remember that brushing twice daily is even more important. Never forget however the neatsfoot oil already recommended, but keep in view that in both feeding and dressing, science is making constant advances, and you should always be on the alert for new ideas.

CHAPTER VII

To show or not to show?

THIS IS A VERY difficult question, as even when you buy a puppy and intend it only for a companion, it may turn out the best of the litter. Along comes some friend and tells you that you have a prospective champion, and you are tempted. The decision lies with you, and of course there are risks, but very much less than one would imagine. However, if you show and do not win, take it philosophically. Both you and your dog need experience and that comes with perseverance. Whether you show your own dog or not, you should support your breed shows, as the day may come when you want another to replace your departed pal, and without shows you would have great difficulty in getting one. There is a great deal of money invested in dogs now-a-days but it is still to a great extent a hobby, and you will meet many nice people in the course of your showing.

The Ruling Body in our country is the Kennel Club, whose present address is 1-4 Clarges Street, Piccadilly, London, W.1. It now also controls Crufts Show, which is held every February. Crufts is the largest Show in the world and in 1961 nearly 8,000 dogs were exhibited there. The Yorkies made a fine display, with all ages, from the puppies just emerging from their black to the seniors in full steel blue.

In addition to watching over the interests of individual owners and breeders, the Kennel Club has regulations governing about 1,800 annual shows. With so many shows available, one is always liable to fall into error over some detail, though with care this need never happen. If you do make a mistake, never try to hide it but inform the ruling body, and you will get courteous and considerate treatment.

The novice would be well advised not to try to start at the top, but begin at the smaller shows. There are now only two

specialist clubs for the breed, *both* in England (*See* Appendix).
An enthusiast will come along some day and start one in
Scotland I hope. However, there is usually a canine society
near at hand that fosters all breeds, and it is useful to join and
meet other dog lovers.

I will now list the various types of Shows, starting with the
smallest.

Classification of Shows

Exemption Classes. A great many Agricultural Shows get
permission to hold four classes for dogs at their annual shows.
If the weather is good, it gives you a pleasant holiday, and, as
entry is on the grounds and your dog need not be registered
at the K.C., you can make up your mind on the spot. However,
if the grass is long and your dog's coat is in good condition –
remember Punch's advice – Don't! You want level ground
to walk your dog on always, with nothing to stick in the coat.
Otherwise show, for your dog will enjoy it, and a slip lead
is all that is wanted.

Sanction Shows. Normally these are confined to members
of a club or society. The Secretary will arrange this for you
and give you a schedule. There is no benching, informality is
the rule, and the Show is held on the Wednesday or Saturday
afternoon. As all varieties compete against each other, and
there is rarely a class for Yorkies, we will take the procedure
step by step, as the routine applies to all shows.

You require a box on which to display your dog to the
Judge; this usually has a glass front, and the little fellow
reposes inside when not actually in action. You can get one
at the local dog shop, or from advertisers in the dog press.
Place your dog on the box and brush every hair into place,
part the hair down his back, look to his head furnishings,
and encourage him. The judge will examine him and probably
lift him up or put him on the table; then he will be walked away
from the judge and to him. Pay special attention to this as it
shows the dog's character. You may have to walk him round

the ring, with other dogs perhaps, and this should be practised at home. Then back to the box, where you brush and put everything straight that the walk may have upset. You compete against all breeds and may perhaps walk beside a St Bernard to the latter's consequent loss of dignity! Champions are barred.

Limited Shows. These are stiffer Sanction Shows and are sure to have a qualifying clause as to area, restriction of classes, area in which exhibitor must reside, or membership of some club, but it is all clearly set out in the schedules. With a little study mistakes are not easy to make. In addition, the secretary wants to make no mistakes at his show, and will give help with the greatest of pleasure, nor will he lose an entry if he can' help it. You may find a class for Yorkies here.

Open Shows. Here any dog may compete, and you will find classes for most breeds. Today Variety Classes are very plentiful, and this is where the management makes ends meet. If there is a class or classes for your breed, someone is responsible for paying the prize money, usually one pound, ten shillings, five shillings, and there will be an entry fee of probably five shillings or six shillings. Unless seven at five shillings or six at six shillings enter, there is a loss, as the Kennel Club sees to it that the prize money is paid in full. Therefore help the show with an entry in each class for your breed, if eligible, and also give one or two to the variety Toy classes. You gain experience, make friends, and may win more than you expended. I have a friend who went to the shows to help his daughter, but her keenness slackened off. He now goes to most Saturday shows, enjoys it and looks on it as his weekly half holiday. In addition always remember that you are helping our four-footed friends.

Championship Shows. These are Open Shows at which the Kennel Club give Challenge Certificates to the best of sex, three of which, awarded under different judges, and, of course, at different shows, give your dog the proud title of Champion. There is no higher title he can get, as British Champion is recognised all over the world. There is a lot of hard work before that stage is reached but it can be done. Opposite page 49 you will find a photograph of six champions owned at the same time by a lady whom I was proud to call friend. She has passed over now and her kennel is ended, but her name and affix of Mrs Crookshank of Johnstounburn will always be remembered in connection with Yorkies. How she loved her dogs, and a win or a loss never put them up or down in her affections.

K.C. Gazette. This monthly is a necessity for the Secretary and the big breeder and exhibitor. It contains all the doings of the Kennel Club, registrations, transfers, exports, etc., forthcoming shows, and any change in rules or definitions. All dogs registered can be traced here, and any mistakes picked up.

K.C. Stud Book. A necessity for all breeders, exhibitors, and secretaries. It contains the records of all Championship Shows and winners, addresses of all secretaries, all prefixes, and a list of those you cannot have, even if applied for. You never know when you may be lured into being an official with all the hard work that entails, and the study of this book will then be of considerable assistance.

Classes at Shows

It should be kept in view that the following information as to classes is correct at the time of going to press. As the Kennel Club is a living body, changes take place from time to time. Therefore before entering for any show the definition should be carefully studied.

You are expected to enter the ring the minute your class is called, so it is necessary to be near it, or to have a friend there to warn you. The show officials do everything possible to see that every dog is in the ring, but if the exhibitor is not known to them and cannot be found, and the dog is not on the bench, the fault lies with the exhibitor.

In any class in which numbers of wins are counted, this holds to the midnight before the date of the show. At the same time, wins in 'Special puppy' and 'puppy' classes do not count.

I give below the normal classes at the big shows. Smaller ones give less, and also the sexes may be *mixed*, which means that a dog and a bitch may compete in the same class. There may be other classes provided, and if you see the word *Special* in front of it, there is a restriction or condition, which needs study as to whether or not you or your dog is eligible. For example, it may be for the *Owner* who has never won a certificate, or for the *Dog* who has not. You read of even hardened exhibitors having their dogs disqualified for digressions, and so the novice must step very carefully.

SPECIAL PUPPY. For dogs of six and not more than nine months on the day of the show.

PUPPY. For dogs of six and not more than twelve months on the day of the show. N.B. A 'special' puppy can compete here.

JUNIOR. For dogs of six and not exceeding eighteen months on the day of the show. N.B. If a dog wins a certain number of prizes before he reaches eighteen months, he may be granted a *Junior Warrant* for this. Application must be made to the Kennel Club for a claim form.

For the next five classes, the winner of a Challenge certificate is barred.

MAIDEN. For dogs not having won a First Prize of the value of One Pound or more.

NOVICE. For dogs which have not won more than three first prizes of the value of one pound or more.

UNDERGRADUATE. For dogs not having won three or more First Prizes of Two Pounds or more.

GRADUATE. For dogs not having won four or more First Prizes of the value of Two Pounds or more in Graduate, Post Graduate, Minor Limit, Mid-Limit, Limit or Open classes.

POST GRADUATE. For dogs which have not won five or more First Prizes of the value of Two Pounds or more in Post Graduate, Minor Limit, Mid-Limit, Limit or Open Classes.

MINOR LIMIT. For dogs not having won two Challenge Certificates or three or more First Prizes in all, each of the value of Two Pounds or more, in Minor Limit, Mid-Limit, Limit or Open Classes.

MID-LIMIT. For dogs not having won three Challenge Certificates or five or more First Prizes, each of the value of Two Pounds or more, in Mid-Limit, Limit or Open Classes.

N.B. A dog may win three Challenge Certificates or more and yet not be a champion, as they were not won under three different judges.

LIMIT. For dogs not having won three Challenge Certificates under three different judges or seven or more First Prizes in all, each of the value of Two Pounds or more, in limit or Open Classes.

OPEN. For all dogs; if confined to a breed or variety, for all dogs of that breed or variety.

N.B. Normally where the First Prize is Two Pounds, it is a Championship Show.
Dachshund is a breed, but there are six varieties – Smooth, Long-coated, and Wire-coated, and a miniature of each.

The Exhibitor

While the dog must always come first, this cannot be assured unless the exhibitor is at ease and without worries. She, and I say this as there are far more lady exhibitors in the ring than men, should see that everything she has on is comfortable, quite apart from fashionable. While I do not agree with the way some turn out in the ring, better that and comfort than to study appearance first. At the benched shows, the strain all day, from the time you and your dog have passed the Vet until you are allowed to depart, is undoubtedly heavy.

The exhibitor should see that she has everything she needs, including the dog's food, which should not be given, unless the judging is very late, until after the judging is over. This self-imposed restriction makes dogs keener, for they would normally have a snooze after a meal. See that the food is something the dog specially likes, and make much of him, win or lose.

Then there is the brush, and the light slip lead. You cannot very well forget the case with the window in which the dog rests and on which he shows off his paces. You also want a dish for water and as soon as possible find out where the tap is, especially if the weather is hot. An old newspaper often comes in handy for wiping up, and takes little space.

Now for you own comfort: take with you a collapsible stool, light and strong, as you cannot stand all day and you cannot be too long away from the bench. There is some discussion going on at the time of writing about stools, chairs and tables blocking up the passages intended for the public to move about in. A little common sense amongst exhibitors would soon shelve this problem. You can brush your dog on your knee or on the upended box, so that a table is not really essential.

Catering at some shows is difficult and means queuing, and this 'time' cannot always be afforded. I would therefore advise you to have in your case a vacuum flask with coffee or tea, and sandwiches. A small cake of soap and a towel, and perhaps a face cloth, will come in handy and take little room. Many people recommend taking a book but from long experience I find that everyone wants to talk 'dog', present, past and future. What is more, as you are a novice you will learn a lot if you remember that you have two ears and two eyes so that your mouth will only give a quarter of the return! Above all do not get rushed but arrive in the ring ready with your dog. There is one way that I have always felt that a novice can learn, and that is to go and spy out the land in advance – at a benched show. See the benches and the people. Then see how they get to the ring and what they do. All the writing in the world will not give you as much confidence as seeing the advice put into practice.

While the above is for benched shows which usually last from ten a.m. to five or six p.m., the unbenched show is different and you have to find yourself a place in the hall, either along the wall or in the ring where you are to show. The time is shorter and you may be able to cut out food, but though the show starts at two p.m. you have no guarantee when it will stop as some judges are very slow (painstaking they call it). I have seen some finish at eight p.m. with everyone left bored stiff, and the bulk of the audience and exhibitors gone. One good thing is that you are usually allowed to leave early after your last class, but if you are unbeaten, it is advisable to wait until the Best in Show is judged for 'one never knows'. Always arrive early so that the Vet can go over your dog without any rush as happens when a lot of dogs arrive together and there is the risk of a snap or a scare. There is always catering at these unbenched shows and usually quick service; there may even be a licence. You can bring your liquid refreshment to your seat.

8. Gloamin Cherry Brandy, Ch. Rose-Petal of Clu-Mor, Ch. The Duchess of Clu-Mor, and Ch. Sorreldene Charley Boy, the best toy team group at the International Kennel Club Chicago Show 1961. Owners Mrs. L. S. Gordon and Miss J. Bennett.

to: Frasie Studio

THE YORKIE IN AMERICA

9. Two delightful champions from the United States.

Photo: Glenview Studio

10. Alice Scott, Mable Ennis with Ch. Lady Roberts of Marcrakit, Judge Col. Ed. McQuown, Mrs Gordon and Ch. Star Twilight of Clu-Mor.

11.   Ch. Hampark Dandy.
Best of Breed at Crufts, 1961 (*see* p. 49 opposite)

12. Six champions, all owned by the late Mrs. Crookshank.
Right: Ch. Mr. Pim, B. Ch. Myrtle, B. Ch. Tufty, B. Ch. Medium, all of Johnstounburn.

Left: Ch. Pimbron and B. Ch. Pipit of Johnstounburn.

CHAMPION HAMPARK DANDY

The property of Mr W. Wilkinson,
135 St. James' Road, Sutton, Surrey.

On the opposite page is a photograph of Best of Breed at Crufts, 1961, who was also, of course, the Certificate winner. He has an interesting story. The owner of the dam is also a Mr Wilkinson, though no relation to Mr W. Wilkinson. He was told by his vet that his bitch should be bred from, and that all bitches should have a litter once, if possible. (The author does not agree with this either on two legs or four). She was accordingly sent to a good, well bred dog and had seven puppies. Hampark Dandy's owner and exhibitor picked him at five weeks old, as the breeder had no special interest in the puppies, beyond following the Vet's advice. I hear you say what a lucky pick, but experience must have counted too as Mr W. Wilkinson had been breeding since 1948.

Hampark Dandy won his

1st Certificate at Windsor under Mrs Stirk, 1960.
2nd Certificate at Bournemouth under Mrs Overett, 1960.
3rd Certificate at Richmond under Miss Noakes, 1960.
4th Certificate at L.K.A., under Mr Joe Braddon, 1960.
5th Certificate at Crufts under Mrs Wood, 1961.

His weight is three-and-a-half pounds, including the bow, and his colours are strictly in conformity with the standard.

PEDIGREE

Sire		
	⌠ Mambo of Tzumiao	⌠ Pagham Sehow Special
Ear-wi-go	⎨	⎨ Pennywort of Pagham
of Tzumiao	⎩ Wee Gem of Gorsecliffe	⎨ Elite of Invincia
		⎩ Victory Lass
Dam		
	⌠ Mitey Joe of the Vale	⌠ Ch Nabish of the Vale
Chota	⎨	⎨ Patricia of the Vale
Memsahib	⎩ Fudge of Bantomy	⎨ Kim of Pooshire
		⎩ Corrie

49

C

CHAPTER VIII

Training on a lead

A<small>S IT IS VERY</small> essential that the show dog should walk and make the most of itself, I think a few hints to the novice may be helpful, as they come from practical experience. Nothing can be more annoying than to see a promising dog lie down in the ring and have to be practically dragged along. On the other hand, a dog can get ideas and no one can understand the sudden change. Once at Crufts, an exhibitor walked his dog away all right, but when half way back the latter balked and sat down. After this had been repeated three times, I changed to the other end of the ring, and he repeated the performance in reverse. Why neither I nor his owner ever understood.

In another case, a lady showed a dog which looked very promising but would not allow itself to be handled by a man. It was erratic in movement. The owner explained that they did not have many visitors, and I suggested taking the dog down to the village 'Local' once or twice a week, where the number of men and loud talk might work a cure. When I met her later at a show where the dog won the certificate, I was told that the dog was now fearless. I merely give these two illustrations to show that any training question must be approached with a very open mind.

My own idea, to start with, is to avoid putting on a lead too early but to let the puppy get past the baby stage to about six months, and then take him outside on the lead but with as little traffic as possible to start with. Speak kindly to him and do not let the lead be jerked. If he hangs back then stop and encourage him and he will come on. He soon becomes used to the lead, which should be hung in a place where he can always see it. The result is that he quickly gets to know that this coming down means a walk with his loved owner, and that is his main pleasure. Having got him used to the lead, then comes the training – on your lawn, if you have one, and if not in some spot in the park, or in a hall if this is possible. The latter is best of all, as most of your shows will be indoors.

One thing I would impress upon the trainer is that there should be no talk during exercise, but as much as you like afterwards. First walk about thirty feet or as near as possible to this range with him on your right side, then about turn and back to where you started. Not more than a dozen times, and less if you find the puppy is getting bored or losing interest. Next, stop once or twice going and coming, and get him to stand showing – but no word of command. When he has done this reasonably well, call it a day, pet him and give him a titbit. Next trial is with him on the left side, as you never know which way the judge will walk them round and there is no rule on this point. Repeat the halts, and each time increase the standing smartly.

If you have another dog, and a friend, the same routine can be carried through with the two later on, so that he has gained experience and knows what is to be done without your having to tell him. It is a bad habit having to give a bit of liver or something similar to make your dog show. Give it to him at the end and he will appreciate it and know what it is given for. Do not tell me a dog does not use his brains, and with your help he will know exactly what should be done in the ring without there being a scene. There is a lot of work and time used in this but I have shown time and again that it can be done if you have the patience and trust. He gets to know that you are depending on him, and will not let you down.

I always like to see the dog that looks up to its owner when it has gone round and up and down, as if to say 'have I done right' and then snuggles up to be lifted on to his perch so that all signs of walking can be brushed out. In other words: You win the prizes at home by training and hard work, and then come into the ring so that the judge may hand out the prizes to you. Take up that attitude and you should get to the top.

Once your dog is trained to this work, it will be helpful to you if you ask a friend to parade the little chap and then study the position, as the judge does. You can then see his faults, if any, and correct them, but *see his faults*, or you will never get anywhere. You have plenty of coat, I hope, and that covers a multitude of sins once your Yorkie is on his box. The heavy number of points for coat and colour will then come into play and make up for any little – and, mind, I say little – slips in the walk. I had a friend in the Cairn ranks, Major Townley, no longer with us, and he could walk into the ring with many of his dogs without lead or any artificial help, and do every-thing described above. His views were the same as mine, with patience and trust in your dog, you made a team.

Perhaps I seem to have gone into this too fully, but I am convinced that the whole secret of success lies here, and in the close attention to detail I urge.

Problem for a Judge

Often when judging, I have to puzzle out a problem. I think this particular one will interest you, and your solution may be the same as mine. It will hammer home my remarks above. Of course exhibitors are not allowed to hold conflab with the judge or to talk to him, other than to reply to any question, but I often wonder whether a reply would have helped the exhibitor, or a question helped the judge.

Two exhibitors were left with their exhibits in the final of the bitch certificate, and neither of the animals had yet been examined. I knew A by sight, but had never handled her bitch; I did not know B nor had I handled her bitch. I went over A's exhibit, and found it good and worth a certificate if the winner, as this statement has to be signed. Then B walked her exhibit round, and then up and down and there was nothing to find fault with. I realised that it was to be a very close decision. I then leant towards this bitch to feel her coat before she went on the table, and it was more good luck than anything else that she did not take my fingers off. I looked at the exhibitor and she appeared genuinely surprised, as I was, so I asked her to put the dog on the table and hoped for the best. It was no use. She was not to be handled by me. So I said to the lady that I was afraid that if I could not examine her exhibit the animal's chance of the certificate was gone – although she looked and moved like a good one. I had another try but it was no good, so A took the certificate and B was reserve. That was the end but I was still worried, since the bitch looked a picture as I sat looking at her idly as the exhibitors moved about and wondered what evil she saw in me. I went over to B and she was quite pleasant. I asked her what bitch it was and she said Champion X. I had heard and read a lot about this bitch and knew she was going to America the following week. I knew one of the judges who had put her up and was sure he would not have done so, if she would not allow herself to be examined. I then said I had often wanted to see X, and her owner replied that she was taken there that day for me to see, in the hope that she would get the certificate as the buyers wanted that. I asked if the bitch had ever behaved like that before – and almost fell through the floor when the reply came 'I have never shown her before, but my husband could not come today'. I said it was a pity she did not tell me, but she replied that she had been told not to speak to the judge, unless to answer a question. I formed my opinion of what had happened at once and still think I was right. I called over a friend, who was one of our crack handlers, and asked if he would take X and walk her along the hall. I then asked B to go to a corner and watch but not show herself. My friend walked the bitch up and down, and put her on the table, without any sign of her biting him. I then went quietly over and offered her the back of my hand as usual and she wagged her tail. I handled her coat, felt her tail, checked her teeth and eyes, placement of ears, and we were the best of friends. This created more interest than the actual judging. I waved the owner over and told her that poor X was not to blame but the exhibitor and the judge for not seeing the position quicker. The little dog had been gallantly defending her 'Missus' from a designing male – and indeed was once more quite willing to see what was inside my skin. The winner came up and asked if I wanted to change my opinion, but I assured them both that I was not now judging dogs, but myself, to see why my long experience had been so slow in getting at the truth.

I, of course, wrote to the American buyers and told them what had taken place – but gave no opinion as to what would happen when and if they had met again – beyond that X was as sound a bitch as I had ever handled. The judge always wants to know why a dog is not making the most of himself and the exhibitor may be able to assist him, but how this could have been done in the case I have recalled, I do not know. If B had said, 'This is Champion X' it would have been a serious breach of regulations, and as it was her first show, she might well have done this. On the whole I think the judge trained and versed in the doggy faith, should have thought quicker and had the bitch showed by a man. 'What would you do, Chum?' as the old junk man used to say on the B.B.C.

CHAPTER IX

Registration and Ownership

THERE ARE MANY pitfalls in the dog world and it may be useful to point out one or two. Ownership is strictly a legal question, but it is wise to consider the Kennel Club attitude.

The Breeder of a dog or litter is the owner at the time of parturition. Note that carefully, as in the States it is the owner of the bitch at the time of service. There is a lot to be said for this view but I merely mention it in passing.

So when you come to register your puppies, you state this fact on the form which you receive from the Kennel Club on application. You pay them a fee of course, at the moment of writing five shillings, and so in the years to come, it can be traced and proved that you were the breeder. If you sell one of your pups, you hand the certificate received from the Kennel Club to the buyer with a transfer form, also obtainable from the Kennel Club and the transaction is complete. If it becomes a Champion, then you can never be robbed of the credit of having bred it, and the Kennel Club will issue a certificate to that effect, if you apply. For very obvious reasons, the Kennel Club will not allow two dogs to have the same name registered in the same breed. To make things easier, a breeder can apply for a *prefix* or *affix*, and this enables names to be picked out quickly. 'Jack' and 'Sandy' have been used up long ago, but if you get 'Timbuctoo', then you can add this to 'Tom', 'Dick', and 'Harry' and have it registered as the dog's name. This is a valuable asset if you are to breed and sell largely. There is a great deal of clerical work in showing, keeping records, correspondence, and a definite system should be adopted to avoid errors.

The forms you get to fill are quite simple if you read them over carefully first, and having completed one, those following are easy. Use *Block Letters* always unless you have a typewriter, and when you sign, if your signature is difficult to read, add your name below. In a transfer, the date is very important as it may involve questions of breeder and shows, so make sure that this is accurate and agreed by both parties.

If you go over the pedigree of Minerva of Johnstounburn opposite you will note below Muffet of Johnstounburn the figures 71790/56, and this is the number she received when registered with the Kennel Club, and every one registered has this and can be traced thereby. Under Champion Pimbron of Johnstounburn however you find K.C.S.B. 1173 AN. This means that his original registration number has been replaced by this one and is an honour, as at a Championship show he must have won a prize in the open class, or if not then he won one in a junior class and was placed reserve for the Challenge Certificate. AN denotes the year 1956, and you will find the shows at which he won and also his full pedigree. This 'Entry to the Stud Book' gives any dog high rank, as you can only get there by merit, and the entry is automatic and not paid for.

MINERVA OF JOHNSTOUNBURN

I give an extended pedigree of the above bitch opposite and it may be helpful to serious breeders to work out how the breeder produced her. I do not do this on highly scientific lines as the average breeder has not the time to read up all that has been written on the subject, and to most it is a hobby that may pay part of its own expenses. Rather I give the idea of how one may study the methods and follow them in so far as they seem to be useful. This method can also be applied in going over other pedigrees. Where you can trace a plan it always means more than a pedigree of the same length without one name ever repeating itself.

Here the repeating factor is Mr Pim of Johnstounburn, who rose to the height of being an international Champion, a tough job. He appears as the paternal grandsire, and as the maternal great grandsire, which is inbreeding to some extent. He is by Parkview Prince out of Flea of Johnstounburn, who

PEDIGREE OF MINERVA OF JOHNSTOUNBURN

Minerva of Johnstounburn

Champion Pimbron of Johnstounburn K.C.S.B. 1173 AN

- *International Champ.* Mr Pim of Johnstounburn
  - Parkview Prince
    - Don Progresso
    - Pat of Atherleigh
  - Flea of Johnstounburn
    - Fairy Prince
    - Fernbank Sandra
- Lady of the Lake
  - Little Tommy Tucker
    - Guinag
    - Avonbridge Titbit
  - Petite Patsy
    - Blue Blazero
    - Pixy of Johnstounburn

Muffet of Johnstounburn 71790/56

- Pimlet of Johnstounburn
  - *International Champ.* Mr Pim of Johnstounburn
    - Parkview Prince
    - Flea of Johnstounburn
  - Laurel Queen
    - Parkview Prince
    - Judy of Crawfords
- Muff of Johnstounburn
  - Invincia Masher
    - Ch Delite of Invincia
    - Margie of Invincia
  - Misty of Johnstounburn
    - Fairy Prince
    - Hazy of Johnstounburn

in turn is by Fairy Prince. One of the great grandparents is Laurel Queen, who also is by Parkview Prince, so that brings in Parkview Prince three times. Flea of Johnstounburn is by Fairy Prince on the paternal side, and sire of Misty of Johnstounburn on the maternal side. The only pity is that we do not have photographs of these dogs as they would give some idea of why they were used for the inbreeding.

You will find that the study is interesting, if not fascinating, and also teaches you much if you follow up on definite lines. You will see in this pedigree Invincia Masher by Ch Delite of Invincia, and then learn that he was the last Champion to be made before the war closed up shows. A daughter of his, Invincia Sun of Victory, won the first post-war bitch certificate. A pleasant pastime for a cold winter's evening.

CHAPTER X

The Yorkie as a Companion

WHILE THE SHOW aspect and all it means is very important, there, is another – that of the companion. I have often heard it remarked that while the Yorkie is an atom of great beauty in the ring, it would not do in the fields. I quite agree, but only up to a point, which is that the coat so carefully brought to perfection could not be risked that way. On the other hand if you want an alert, keen, observant little pal, then get hold of the bigger ones, from seven to eight pounds, or the pup that is being sold by a well-known breeder who thinks it will be too big for show. You will get friendly breeders who will do this and give you the benefit of their experience. If you can get it under six months, you are on the sure road to success, but if older than that, you will have more work in turning its affections to you.

While definitely bought for other than show, you could always try it at the small sanction show, to lead others to see what a fine little companion he makes, with his coat and furnishings half way to the ground only, and an asset in the car with his little bootees on.

Though a Toy, he is also a terrier, so you can have little fear of his pluck and abilities to walk you for many a happy mile. Of course you do not brush the coat daily to increase its length, but you keep it medium short and off the ground, a brush on return from a walk that has been a joy, being all that is needed. The head hair (technicalities omitted in this chapter) is kept similarly, as the little fellow will stick his head into every rabbit and rat hole he sees, and this keeps the growth down.

I have heard it said that the Yorkie does not live as long as other dogs, but I have never obtained a proper explanation of this story. My knowledge of the average age is culled from breeders in all the countries, and twelve to fifteen years is not looked on as a rarity, while I have seen them over ten and still quite fit to risk at a small show with some hope of winning. If you walk them as I say, and of course in reasonable weather, you must be a little more lavish with the food as there is a lot of energy used, and that must be made up. I do not match them for strength against the Foxie or the Cairn, but they can do three to five miles daily and both of you will benefit from it.

I will quote an actual case. In walking from the Burgh to our little house which is in the country, I noted for over a year a Yorkie, who was a little 'rascal', and dreaded that one fine day he would be killed by the passing traffic, as his home was at the corner leading from the main road. Now he is still in his hey-day, eight years old and nine pounds weight, very friendly and the cutest traffic dodger I know. He is not a show specimen being high enough on the leg, and short of coat, though having a genuine pedigree. He goes with his owner anywhere, and is quite obedient, but he knows far more ways of getting out of the house, than getting in! There is heavy traffic of all sorts both ways, and you know the interest every dog has in every car wheel. Every car that stops on either side of the road has to be duly checked, all four wheels if stopped long enough, and then he returns to his base if his owners are not waiting for him. Otherwise he makes the other side his base. He checks if a car is coming the other way, and allows it to pass, and then over like a streak. The highlight of his week is when he gets a walk in 'The Dell', and of course he goes into the burn if he gets half a chance! Intelligence to the heels, a bit naughty you may say, and he may be killed some day, but he loves life and his owners, and is a wonderful guard for giving warning. That is all one could ask of a dog of that size.

If you do not want the nerve-racking show dressings, and still hanker after a Yorkie, you can do a lot worse than a Yorkie of seven to nine pounds or more and kept in short coat.

This little fellow answers to the name of 'Kim', and I have

learned that he is a very keen rat killer and goes round all the farms with his master when the Corn Stacks are being thrashed. Each stack has a surround of wire netting put up so that the rats cannot escape, and he, and any other terriers that want a day's work, are put inside the netting. I have seen thirty rats laid out after the stack is ended. Usually one bite settles the dispute, but often the rat turns and bites, and at the end of the day, the little fellow has quite a few scars to be disinfected. This proves that the rat killing propensities of the days of Huddersfield Ben, are still inherited by the Yorkie of today.

CHAPTER XI

The Rise of the Yorkie

WHEN WAR BROKE OUT in 1939, all shows stopped at once and it is interesting, in all breeds, to observe the gap this made in the production of show specimens. The Yorkie came out of it well as, with one exception, all the dogs and bitches with challenge Certificates managed to obtain their third, and so the title Champion, before the curtain fell at Kensington Canine Show, judged by Mr McCandlish. The winners were – in dogs Ch Delite of Invincia; Ch Chilawee of Soham; and in bitches Benedetta of Soham. The winner of one certificate was Beelzebub, and when the war ended and the shows got started again, he did not appear in the K.C. awards.

The great benefit of the clubs to the breeds was well exemplified here as, owing to destroyed benching, etc, the big shows could not get started quickly, whereupon the clubs stepped into the breach. The Yorkshire Terrier Club ran two shows, both in London, the first judged by Lady Edith Windham Dawson who awarded the dog certificate to Ben's Blue Pride, and the bitch to Invincia Sun of Victory – a daughter of Ch Delite the last prewar dog champion. The second, judged by Mrs Clenshaw, gave Blue Pride his second certificate, while Lady Nada got her first. It is worthy of note that only one of these winners was champion bred and there were a few unregistered in the back blood. This seems to me to show that there is a great deal of good Yorkshire blood that is not registered at the time, but traced back when the full pedigree of a good winner is wanted. However, they were now started again, and next year (1947) the shows were getting into their stride, as in addition to the Club Show, four others were held and Blue Pride became the first postwar Champion. At the same show appeared Veeplustoo of Achmonie, a bitch who took the three certificates of the year and the title of champion.

Sad to relate the other two certificates were withheld by the judges at the two remaining shows. Wee Don of Antherleigh won two dog certificates, and Starlight one.

Here it will be advisable to touch on the number of dogs registered at the Kennel Club as this is a more reliable test of the popularity of a dog than the number at a show. The latter can be affected by the popularity or otherwise of the judge, the accessibility of the venue of the show, or the time of the year. Prior to the year 1939, the year of the war, the average for the five years was 250 registrations per annum, while 1939 gave 147, a drop. 1940 only produced forty-seven, the lowest ever, and the worst was then feared for the breed. 1941 gave fifty-six registrations; 1942 – 132; 1943 – 236; 1944 – 366; while 1945 produced the then extraordinary figure of 479; breaking all possible records, as was then thought, 1946 gave 727; however 1947, the year of the first post war shows described previously, gave 953, and the Yorkie was safe. Fortunately nothing stands still – and the Yorkie was to go on to new heights, though few realised it.

I propose now to give the highlights of the shows and registrations down to the last records issued by the Kennel Club. They make wonderful reading for the Yorkie lover. They also will give the novice an insight into the ups and downs in the show ring, the brilliant success, the tragic failure, and the firm determination of the exhibitors that the breed is to go on and keep its place as the best British Toy dog.

In 1948, the registrations fell to 931, but the number of shows giving certificates for the breed rose to sixteen, and only these are dealt with in the next few pages. Starlight completed his title, and Wee Don of Atherleigh did likewise, capturing seven certificates in the year. In bitches Ch Veeplustoo continued her career with four certificates out of seven shows; Ch Hebsonian Jealousy did seven shows and took six – a wonderful record, with Ch Kelbro Minnie taking three certificates out of six shows.

In 1949, the registrations for the first time got into four figures, at 1,041, and have kept there ever since. There were eighteen shows, and Ch Splendour of Invincia put up the marvellous record of going to eleven of them and taking home eleven certificates, having had two in the previous year. This did not leave much for the others, but Ch Wee Don of Atherleigh took two of them. In bitches Ch Tufty of Johnstounburn took five certificates in six attempts, while Ch Veeplustoo took three out of three, good work. Ch Hebsonian Jealousy got two certificates out of three, following up her 1948 success.

We can discuss a point here in view of the above successes – should champions be allowed to compete against ordinary dogs once they have got their title. There are many ways of looking at this but mine is quite simple. The Kennel Club say here is a certificate and the judge has to sign it to confirm that the dog getting it is worthy of being a champion. It is open to any dog of any age and has been won by puppies, and especially is this the case in Shetland Sheep Dogs. The effect of this is that it makes it more difficult for any dog to win the title Champion. Is that not what we want – sound, solid Champions and not cheap Champions – and what more heart-warming than to beat a tried and well-known Champion. Where any other system is used you find far more champions every year. So you can think it out, but to my mind the Champion says, 'let them all come and I will beat them,' but sometimes he does not and a new one arises.

In 1950, registrations rose to 1,217. In dogs, in nineteen shows, Ch Martynwyns Surprise of Atherleigh collected five certificates, while Mr Pim of Johnstounburn took four and the title, and Ch Splendour took 4, showing what a stayer he was. Bitches were not so good, but Ch Wee Gertrude took two.

In 1951 registrations (1,331) were still rising and there were twenty-two shows, but nothing very startling resulted, except that Ch Martynwyns Surprise came out once more and took seven certificates straight off – a brilliant performance. This is more wonderful when you learn that in 1949, he made seven appearances and could get no nearer to a certificate than reserve. Think this out in connection with my earlier remarks on champions, and it will interest you. The following bitches took three each, and the title – Feona of Phylreyne, Camellia Hopwood, Martynwyns Golden Girl and Titania of Invincia.

In 1952, there was a slight recession in registrations at 1,241 but competition at the twenty shows was heavy, seven champions appearing at various times. Ch Eoforwic Envoy of Yadnum appeared thirteen times, while the total number of shows was twenty. He took three certificates however. Ch Sunstar of Invincia took four in five appearances, good work. In bitches, the best performance was that of Ch Winpal Henrietta, with five certificates out of seven shows.

In 1953, registrations were only seven up at 1,248, but there were twenty-one shows. The dog of the year was Ch Stirkean's Chota Sahib, who appeared twice last year and took one certificate, but made every one sit up by taking six from seven appearances this year. Bitches however showed the keenness of competition as Ch Medium of Johnstounburn turned out fourteen times to get four certificates; Ch Fay of Phylreyne, nine times for three; and Ch Aerial of Winpal eight times for three.

In 1954, registrations jumped fourteen, and have been rising every year since. Shows dropped to nineteen, as some old-established ones could not carry on. Ch Blue Simon appeared once in 1953 with no success in certificates, but had improved beyond measure, so came out ten times and took eight certificates, a very creditable performance. In eight attempts, Ch Midnight Gold of Yadnum took three certificates running and the title. In bitches, Ch Aerial of Winpal added four to her record out of six tries, while Ch Myrtle of Johnstounburn in five tries added three to her total of six.

In 1955 the registrations rose to 1,708, with twenty shows. Competition, especially in dogs, was heavy. Ch Burghwallis Little Imp appeared eleven times taking four certificates; Ch Epperstones Bon Ton six for five; Ch Stirkean's Kandy Boy six for five; thus leaving six for the rest. Then there was the tragedy of Ch Midnight Gold of Yadnum who came out nine times, yet while never far from the top, he did not receive a single certificate, showing how a dog can go off colour. The certificates for bitches were more spread out, as Ch Wee Mischief took three from three, to add to her two in 1954; Ch Martynwyns Adora took three from seven tries to add to her one of 1954; while Ch Medium of Johnstounburn only received one from eight shows. Of course bitches are always more tricky than dogs for show, as there is 'season' and maternal duties to keep in view.

In 1956, history was made as registrations reached 2,148. When you compare this with the 147 of 1939, you will see the tremendous advance made in a little over fifteen years. The shows were twenty as in the previous year, and the outstanding dog was Ch Pookshill Hilaire of Erlcour who won the title and six certificates in eight shows. Pimbron of Johnstounburn appeared at twelve shows, but only managed two certificates, while Efferstones Bon Ton took two from three tries. Again the bitch certificates were spread out with Ch Pipit of Johnstounburn taking four from ten appearances, and Symon's Querida of Tolestar two from seven, just missing the title. Ch Buranthea's Angel Bright did better with four from five tries. Of the other ten certificates one bitch won two while all the rest went in ones.

In 1957, registrations again increased to 2,313, and the shows to twenty-one. Ch Moonglow of Yadnum, who in 1956 won his title and three certificates out of five tries, turned out ten times this year to take six certificates and prove that he was a star turn. Ch Pimbron of Johnstounburn took two certificates from six appearances and June's Boy the same number from seven. In bitches there was one tragedy, as Elaine of Astolat turned out at nine shows but did not receive one certificate although always in the running. What a plucky owner to 'stick it out'. Ch Blue Orchid of Hilfore got three out of seven attempts; Ch Martini four out of the same number; and Ch Cressida of Erlcour made it five out of seven. That left nine for the dozens of other triers.

In 1958 we near the end of the account with 2,824 registrations and twenty-three shows. Competition in dogs was bitter. Ch Ravelin's Gaiety Boy who took one certificate in three tries in the previous year turned out seven times and took five certificates to prove he was no flash in the pan. Sir Lancelot of Astolat, tried five times in 1957 without success but this year he won his title and three certificates out of ten attempts. Ch Societyrow Dog Friday took his title and three certificates in five tries. Buranthea's Doutelle took two out of nine attempts, and I may say now that in the following year he took one out of three and thus clinched the title of Champion. In bitches the competition was very strong and few certificates for many attempts was the order of the year. Ch Coulgorm Chloe four certificates out of ten shows; Ch Deedees Stirkeans Faustina four out of nine; Ch Stirkeans Rhapsody four out of eight; and Elaine Of Astolat two out of fourteen.

In 1959, registrations rocketed to 3,244, while shows still stood at twenty-three. Four dogs took seventeen of the certificates leaving six for the others. Ch Don Carlo of Progresso won eight out of nine tries; Ch Pedimins Piper got four out of nine; Ch Stirkeans Astonoffs Horatio three out of ten; and Burghwallis Vikki two out of eight. In bitches, two of the entries took seventeen certificates between them, whereas it took four to achieve this among the dogs. Ch Deedees Stirkeans Faustina continued her winning ways by taking twelve certificates out of fifteen attempts while Ch Pagnell Prima Donna of Wiske took five out of twelve. There is one case of perseverance that must be recorded, as Elaine of Astolat won her title of champion with one certificate out of four shows. In the previous year she had taken two certificates from fourteen shows. I take my hat off to the owner for knowing she had a good bitch and, once started, never flinching at defeat until the bitch scored her final success.

This brings us to the end of the road so far as records officially issued by the Kennel Club in their Stud books are concerned. Details for 1960 will not be received until late in 1961, as the latter are a monumental work. One thing I am sure of, however, is that registrations will break all records at over 4,000, as they numbered 3,633 up to November, and the average is about 400 a month. 1960 indeed brought to the top Britain's own Toy Dog, the Yorkie.

CHAPTER XII

The Yorkie in Scotland

WHEN I CAME SOUTH in 1920, I found a very keen band of breeders in Edinburgh, with a very strong hand in Yorkshire Terriers, though other Toys had their adherents. That they knew what they were doing was clear from the fact that they produced some half a dozen or so Champions, no mean feat in a country where there are never more than half a dozen championship shows per annum and usually less. One of that band was Miss Souter who is still with us and as enthusiastic as ever. Her name is now Mrs Lowrie, but her prefix of Lilyhill has never changed. Then she had Champions Supreme, Mademoiselle and Angelina, while Blue Iris had two certificates, all of them Lilyhills; Mrs. White's Ch Grindlay Sensation; Mrs McCraw's Ch Blenheim Prince; and Mrs Hunter's Hullard Supreme, with two certificates when showing closed down owing to the war, all went to show that Scotland still supported the dog she undoubtedly helped to produce.

Then came the war and stocks gradually died down and only a few were able to survive the struggle. Many were the fears that the old days and dogs were things of the past. This idea was quickly exploded however as Mrs Pannett came out and won the title for Firhill Fairy, while Mrs Crookshank brought the Johnstounburns to the top, and actually held six Champions at the one time (*See* Plate 12) Mr Pim; Myrtle; Tufty; Medium; Pipit; and Pimbron. The loss her death caused to the breed in Scotland will take a long time to make up. Miss Hill's Wee Spunkie helped by winning two certificates.

Of course Mrs Lowrie seldom misses any show to keep the breed before the public in Scotland, and can go down into England and win there. Since the war there has been a big change in show days and there are few held in mid-week, but often half a dozen on Saturday afternoon, in various parts of Scotland. England being bigger naturally has far more. Each Club is allowed two shows, one in each half of the year, and the tendency is to have more classes for every variety of dog than classes for one breed of dog. This puts the Yorkie at a decided disadvantage, but enables the show to come out without a loss. Unless the judge knows the Yorkie and has studied its good and bad points, it is overlooked in a big Variety Class (thirty or more all sorts), and unless there is a goodly number of them forward to impress the judge and public, there is no prize for the odd one. The remedy lies in the hands of owners who can put in an appearance when the show is near at hand. This also applies to other breeds, but there are very few breeds so distinctive as the Yorkie, and he is one of the very few all British Toys left to us. Too often does a 'foreigner' get well placed and even best in show, after a few years in the country. Why this should be I leave you to think out, as the judges normally have not been in the country of origin.

CHAPTER XIII

The Yorkie in America

IT WAS VERY SURPRISING to learn recently that the only dog to surpass the Yorkie in number of Exports was the Poodle. He is exceedingly popular in the United States and the number of British Champions to acquire the American and Canadian title also is surprising. I went over a list of Champions of the last few years and found that there were almost 250. Of course their system out there is different from ours, but their country is bigger. Eight is about the most we could make in a year. Mrs Gordon and Miss Scott in partnership imported a champion dog from Eire and he produced some fourteen champions for them, in addition to this record of 104 times best of breed, besides other prizes. An amusing fact is that one of these Champions came into existence through a grandmother giving her grand-daughter a present of a bitch when she was just five years old. This bitch when mated produced Ch Bobo's Bonny, so that this little girl was the owner and breeder of a champion at six years. Her name is Miss Suzanne Peterson. I could fill a book with the names of keen breeders, and importers. Take Mrs S. E. Ferguson of Lake Genva, Wis, with fourteen champions to her credit. Then Mrs Stella Myers, Los Angeles, with three champions and two of them Obedience winners also, to prove they have brains. Then Mrs Theron Trudgian, Denver, with six, and a bitch with the record for being the winner of twelve groups. Mrs Fred Rice, Los Angeles has been breeding since 1899, and has seven champions to her credit and all very tiny. Mrs Iola Suhr is known for half a dozen champions, but particularly for one bitch that has produced champions in every litter, while many bitches sold have gone on producing champions. Had I space I could say more, as the Americans deserve it for the way they have kept on with the Yorkie and stuck to the standard. If they thought they were slipping, another was imported to put matters right.

Records published by the Great Dog Historian
Edward C. Ash, M.R.A.C.

About 1892, Mrs Troughear's Conqueror was sold to an American lady,Mrs Wimot, the wife of an actor, for £250. He weighed five-and-a-half pounds. But his coat was exceptional, for on his body it was twenty-six inches long, on his head twenty-three-and-a-half inches, and below the eye and muzzle eighteen-and-a-half inches.

Mrs Foster's kennel was making great headway in the meantime and her little Ch Ted actually beat the famous Bulldog, British Monarch, in a variety class, as well as some of the leading St Bernards. This little fellow won nearly 300 prizes and was the Yorkie of his day.

About that time Mrs Foster also brought out Bradford Marie. Healthy and lively, the latter only weighed one pound fourteen ounces. Owing to the illness of her owner, Marie was sold for £100, but did not live more than seven or eight months with her new owner. These small dogs are so concentrated in everything that they can easily die of a broken heart. Mrs Foster also owned Bradford Queen of the Toys, not so famous on the show bench as Marie, but weighing only twenty-four ounces. This is the smallest Yorkie yet recorded.

Prior to 1931, Mr Ash considered that the leading Yorkies were Sprig of Blossom, winner of sixteen Challenge Certificates; Mr J. Hardman's kennel with Overdale Regenta; and Mr J. Wood with Armley Roy. Mr Scollay owned the remarkable Mendham Peggy and Mr H. Lemon, Boy Blue. What strikes me most about the breed is the number of winning and Championship dogs that have no championships in their back blood to the third or fourth generation. In many breeds you see the winners with as much red ink in their pedigrees as would float a battleship. Red ink is used to call attention to the title, and no doubt does impress the novice, although it has the opposite effect on me in any breed.

Yorkshire Terrier Clubs

The Yorkshire Terrier Club

    Secretary: Miss P. Noakes, 106 Browning Road, Manor Park, London, E.12.

The Northern Counties Terrier Club

    Secretary: Mrs A. Swan, 76 Stockport Road, Bredbury, Cheshire.

GLOSSARY

BAT EARS	Large and with rounded points.
BEARD	The longish hair from the underjaw.
B.B.	Best of Breed.
B.I.S.	Best in Show.
B.O.S.	Best Opposite Sex.
B.S.	Best of Sex, which carries the C.C., that is the Challenge Certificate, at a championship show.
BLOOM	Usually 'in full-bloom' – perfect condition in body and especially coat.
BRISKET	The body immediately in front of the chest and between the forelegs.
CAESAREAN	An operation performed by a Vet to save the dam's life where normal parturition is impossible. It can be done and the litter saved, but not recommended, and a foster mother must be on hand.
COUPLED	Refers to the length between the limb joints – used as long or short coupled.
COW-HOCKED	When the hocks are bent inwards and almost touching, as in cows.
DAM	Female, usually applied to the mother of puppies.
DEW CLAWS	Rudimentary toes on the inside of the hind legs below the hocks, not uncommon.

DOMED SKULL	Also apple head, a rounded skull, instead of flat. A fault in a Yorkie.
ELBOW	The joint at the top of the foreleg.
GAY	Applied to the tail when carried too high or over the back – a Yorkie's should be horizontal.
FALL	The hair of the head from the top of the skull, should be long right down the muzzle, and includes the moustache; a foot long is not very uncommon.
FEATHERING	The hair at the back of the legs.
FRONT	The forelegs and chest.
HEAT	And 'Season', expression for when the bitch is ready to breed.
HOCKS	Hind leg joint below the stifles.
MOUSTACHE	See Fall, hair from upper lips.
MUZZLE	Includes mouth and nose below the eye.
OCCIPUT	The bony prominence on the top of the skull.
OVERSHOT	The upper teeth, and/or jaw projecting over the lower.
PASTERN	The leg below the knee or hock.
PIGJAWED	Rather uncommon and means being excessively over-shot.
PUPPY	Normally a dog under a year for showing purposes, but under six months for licensing.
ROACH	Curved back like the Bedlington or Whippet but very undesirable in a Yorkie.
SIRE	The father of a puppy or litter.
SOOTY	Dark hair mingled with the tan – see standard – a bad fault in a Yorkie.
STOP	The depression between the eyes.
UNDERSHOT	The teeth and/or jaw projecting beyond the upper, the opposite of overshot.
WITHERS	The ridge between the shoulder blades at the root of the neck – where height is usually measured.

Index

Age, 59, 60
Albert, 12
America, 70

Birmingham, 12
Black Puppies, 36
Block Letters, 56
Blue Scotch, 12
Bootees, 38
Box for Show, 42, 47
Broken Haired Terriers, 12
Bruce, 13
Brushes, 38

Championship Shows, 43
Change in Colour, 37
Charlie, 13
Classes at Shows, 45
Clydesdale Terriers, 11, 14
Coat Specifics, 39
Cobden, 14
Companion Dog, 60
Crack, 13
Cremorne, 12
Crib, 13
Cropping, 37

Dew Claws, 37
Dinsdale, Mr, 12
Dip in Back, 21
Docked Tails, 37
Drying, 28
Dundreary, 13

Ears, Cut, 12
Ears, Uncut, 12
Eden, Mr, 13
Exemption Classes, 42

Fall, 38, 73
Feeding, 39
Foster, Mr, 13
Foster, Mrs, 13
Foster Mothers, 36

Gruel, 35

Huddersfield Ben, 11, 16

Islington, 12

Jimmy, 13
Junior Warrant, 42

Kennel Club, 41
Kennel Club Gazette, 44
Kennel Club Stud Book, 44

Limited Shows, 43
Little Kate, 14

Maltese, 14
Marples, Theo, 19
Mask, 38
Mixed Classes, 45
Mossy, 12
Moustaches, 38, 73
Mozart, 14

Neatsfoot Oil, 38
Newcastle, 12

Open Shows, 43
Ownership, 55

Paisley Terriers, 11, 14
Parting in Coat, 38
Pearce, Frank, 12
Prefixes, 55
Prince, 12

Rearing and Training, 37, 50
Records, 33
Registration, 55
Rinsing, 38
Roach Back, 21

Sanction Shows, 42
Scotch Terriers, 12

Scotland, 69
Shows, 42
Sooty, 15, 17
Special Classes, 45
Stables, Dr Gordon, 11
Standard, Official, 17

Tiny, 14

Tissue Paper, 38
Tom, 13

Wallet, 14
Washing, 38
Wattie, 13

Yorkie Clubs, 74